LIFE IN
THE MILL

ANTHONY BURTON

IMPORTANT DATES

1589 The Revd William Lee invents a machine for knitting hosiery.

1724 Thomas Lombe establishes a mill in Derby for spinning silk.

1733 John Kay invents the flying shuttle that greatly speeds up work on the loom.

1764 James Hargreaves invents the spinning jenny, which enabled one operative to do the same amount of work as many workers using the traditional methods.

1771 Richard Arkwright establishes a cotton mill at Cromford in Derbyshire, using his newly invented spinning machinery powered by waterwheel. Cromford becomes the first mill town.

1779 Samuel Crompton invents the spinning mule, a machine that combines the best features of Hargreaves' and Arkwright's machines.

1786 Dr Edmund Cartwright invents the first automatic loom.

1788 The first steam engine is installed to provide power for a cotton mill at Papplewick, Nottinghamshire.

1798 Robert Owen arrives to take over the cotton mills at New Lanark in Scotland and begins a social experiment to improve the conditions of the workers.

1801 Joseph Marie Jacquard invents a new type of loom for the silk industry that uses punched cards to create elaborate patterns.

1806 Gas lighting is introduced into cotton mills for the first time.

1811 The beginnings of Luddism: framework knitters in Nottingham and Leicester begin smashing machines, with the movement's leaders appearing under the name of 'General Ludd'.

1819 The Cotton Mills and Factories Act makes it illegal to employ mill apprentices under the age of nine and limits working hours to 16 a day.

1828 The ring spinning frame is invented in America; by the 20th century it dominates factory spinning.

1833 The Factory Act becomes the first general legislation on the work of children in every industry, limiting the age at which they can start and the hours they can work.

1847 The Ten Hour Act is passed.

1856 William Henry Perkin develops the first aniline dye for silk.

1861 The start of the American Civil War causes a cotton famine in Lancashire.

1904 Courtaulds acquire the UK rights to Cross and Bevan's cellulose treating process and use it to develop the artificial fibre, rayon.

1937 W.H. Carothers develops a new artificial fibre, nylon.

1950 Introduction of the Sulzer shuttleless loom.

1983 First electronic Jacquard loom introduced in Milan.

2001 New Lanark and the Derwent Valleys are made World Heritage Sites in recognition of their importance in the textile revolution.

THE TEXTILE REVOLUTION

Traditionally the British textile industry was based on wool. At the beginning of the 16th century the human population of England was estimated at three million, but the country supported eight million sheep. Most of the wool went for export, with merchants coming from as far away as Italy to buy fleeces; areas such as the Cotswolds and East Anglia grew prosperous on the trade. The results can still be seen in the magnificent 'wool churches' that even quite modest towns and villages were able to afford to build. A proportion of the wool was kept in Britain for making into yarn, to be used for knitting or weaving. Some cotton cloth was also produced, but it was mostly for comparatively modest uses, such as linings for the better class of garments. All that began to change when the British began trading with India.

By the middle of the 17th century cotton cloth was being imported into Britain. Not everyone approved of the importing of foreign cloth: the author Daniel Defoe ridiculed the new fashion, writing caustically of 'ladies of quality dressed in Indian carpets' which previously their chambermaids would have thought 'too ordinary for them'. However, the new, brightly patterned material called calico, after the port of Calicut, proved hugely popular with many people. British manufacturers were beginning to think that they could make far bigger profits by importing the raw cotton instead of finished cloth, and spinning and weaving it themselves. This called for improvements in productivity to meet the increased demand.

The first step forward came in 1733 when John Kay of Bury, Lancashire, invented his flying shuttle. The shuttle carries the weft thread, and is passed from one side of the loom to the other, interweaving with the fixed thread, the warp. Kay's invention replaced the human hands of the weaver with mechanical hands, operated by cords, and the shuttle ran on wheels. It enabled one weaver to do the work of two. What was needed now was new machinery to increase the production of yarn. Solving that problem began an industrial revolution.

▼ The early cotton mills imitated the successful calicos imported from India by printing designs onto the finished cloth.

A COTTAGE INDUSTRY

The woollen industry was a complex one that involved very large numbers of people. A writer in 1715 calculated that turning 240lbs (109kg) of wool into cloth would employ 132 people for a week. The process began with the clothier who bought the fleeces; he either got them direct from the farmer or waited until they had been sorted and then obtained them from one of the trade centres, or from 'braggers' who attended country fairs. The fleeces had to be cleaned and scoured, usually by washing in a stream and treating with urine to remove the grease. After they had been dried they could either be dyed immediately, which ensured that the colour ran through every strand – hence the term a 'dyed in the wool villain' means a villain through and through – or dyed 'in the piece' after weaving. The wool at this stage was still tangled and needed to be straightened out. There were various methods for achieving this, including scribbling (a system similar to carding but used for coarse fibre) and combing, which were carried out under the clothier's supervision.

A FAMILY AFFAIR

Combing usually took place in the combers' own homes. This involved the whole family – father, mother and children – sitting round the comb-pot full of wool, that was heated by charcoal. It gave off noxious fumes, so that one contemporary noted combers were 'not living half their days'. The wool often went direct to a weaver and his family for carding. The carding process was often the work of the youngest child. It involved pulling the wool between cards, similar to large table-tennis bats studded with wire. This aligned the fibres ready for spinning, which was generally women's work, hence the word 'spinster'.

SPINNING AND WEAVING

Spinning consists of two basic operations, stretching the fibres out and then twisting them

▼ Carding and spinning in a Shetland croft: the woman on the left is carding the wool, which is then passed to the woman with the spinning wheel.

▲ A Lancashire handloom weaver using a flying shuttle, which is sent from side to side by jerking the stick held in his right hand.

▲ Dyeing was often carried out by specialists or, as here, as part of a mill complex. It involved immersing the yarn or the cloth in steaming vats.

together to form yarn. Most people today are familiar with the spinning wheel, but in the 17th century many spinsters used a far larger wheel, up to 5 feet (1.5m) tall. The yarn was then passed to the weaver, usually the man of the house.

When weaving, one set of threads, the warp, has to be arranged on the loom, threaded through a mechanism that allows alternate threads to be raised and lowered. The shuttle, carrying the weft thread, is then thrown through the gap, and the weft battened home. When making broadcloth, the loom was too wide for one man to manage easily, so it became customary for one of the sons of the house to help. The weaver would throw the shuttle across and the boy would return it for the next line. The flying shuttle did away with the work of the youngster. Cloth making was very much a family affair, and the weavers cherished their independence. There was a tradition of honouring 'Saint Monday': taking the day off and making up the time by working late on other days.

FULLING AND CROPPING

Next the cloth needed to be cleaned and shrunk, and this was usually carried out in a fulling mill. The cloth was soaked in water and fuller's earth to remove grease and was then pounded by giant hammers powered by a waterwheel. At the end of the process it was stretched out on a tenter frame and kept taut by hooks, which is why anyone feeling tense is said to be on tenterhooks. The final stage was to raise the nap of the cloth by brushing it with teazles, after which it could be smoothed by cropping with giant shears. Cropping was a highly skilled operation and the croppers or cloth dressers were amongst the most highly paid of all cloth workers. The finished cloth was now ready for sale, often being sent to one of the great markets, such as the Piece Hall in Halifax, Yorkshire.

WARP AND WEFT

An old weavers' joke helps everyone remember which is which on the loom: 'The warp goes up and down, and the weft goes from weft to wight.'

ARKWRIGHT OF CROMFORD

▲ A 1790 portrait of Sir Richard Arkwright (1732–92), showing him with a model of his waterframe.

▼ An engraving of a cotton mill, from a 19th century encyclopedia: the carding engines, used for aligning the fibres, can be seen on the left.

The increased productivity in weaving and the new demand for cotton cloth created a need to find a more efficient spinning system. The first major advance came when James Hargreaves (1720–78) invented the spinning jenny in 1764. It was essentially quite a simple device. The old spinning wheel was put on its side and used to turn a number of spindles instead of just one. It met initial opposition from spinners who, fearing for their livelihood, attacked and destroyed some machines, while the more ruthless clothiers simply pirated the idea. The spinning jenny resulted in increased production, but no real social change: it was hand operated and could be set up in any simple workshop. The next spinning machinery, invented by Richard Arkwright in 1769, was very different.

Arkwright began his working life as a barber and wig-maker in Preston, Lancashire, and he would certainly have heard plenty of conversation about the need for new machinery as he snipped away at his customers' hair. His ideas were not entirely new – two other inventors, John Wyatt and Lewis Paul, had tried something similar – but represented a totally new approach to the industry. He introduced two innovations. First he replaced the hand cards with a carding engine, in which the cotton was passed over rollers studded with wire. For spinning

➤ An original Arkwright waterframe used for spinning cotton, now on display at Helmshore Textile Museum in Lancashire.

he built a machine that passed the loosely aligned cotton from the carding engine through rollers moving at different speeds to draw out the threads. From here the stretched threads passed down to a rotating flyer that twisted them together. The big difference was that these were not machines that could be hand operated: they were to be powered by waterwheel, thus the spinning machines came to be known as 'waterframes'. And so it was that the tasks of carding and spinning were about to be taken out of the home and placed in a factory.

A MOVE TO CROMFORD

Arkwright knew that if he started his first mill in Lancashire it would probably suffer the same fate as the jenny, either being smashed or pirated – or both. So, after initial trials in Nottingham, he decided in 1771 to move to the Derbyshire hamlet of Cromford. There was no fear of opposition here, but neither was a large workforce available; Arkwright not only had to build a mill, he also had to build the first mill village. Many of the houses, such as those on North Street, survive and they have the distinctive long weavers' windows on the top floor, showing where looms would be set to work. The work largely went to children, aged between seven and 13, who worked 13 hours a day.

The Cromford mill represented a social as well as an industrial revolution. Women and children in the textile industry were used to hard work and long hours, but they worked in the familiar surroundings of their own homes and set their own timetables.

⌃ One of the terraced houses in North Street, Cromford, built by Arkwright for his workers. The long windows on the upper floor indicate that the building was used for weaving, rather than accommodation.

Now when the factory bell rang everyone had to be at their place, and there they stayed until the waterwheel was stopped and the machines came to a standstill.

Arkwright's initial fears about Lancashire were justified. When a mill was built using his machinery near Chorley, the locals burned it to the ground. They threatened to march on Cromford, so Arkwright prepared for the worst, building a formidable arsenal including small arms and cannon. The rioters never came. Arkwright prospered, was knighted and lived out his days in a grand mansion, Willersley Castle, overlooking the mill where his fortune was being made.

YEARS OF INVENTION

▲ New spinning mules being installed in a Gloucestershire woollen mill in the early 20th century.

Arkwright was not the only one thinking about improvements. Samuel Crompton was born in Lancashire in 1753. His father died when he was just five years old, and he was soon having to contribute to the family income by working as a weaver. But he was also a boy of many interests. He went to evening classes in Bolton, and when he developed an interest in music but did not have the money to buy an instrument, he made his own violin. Arkwright's machine was successful, but it did not produce very fine or very even yarn. Crompton took elements from both the waterframe and the jenny and combined them to create a hybrid, hence the name – spinning mule. It used rollers, again, to draw out the thread, which then passed to rows of spindles attached to a moving carriage. As the carriage moved away from the roller, so the yarn was stretched even finer. The spindles rotated to give the twist. The tension was then released and the carriage rolled back towards the rollers, winding on the yarn. The mule was a great success, and Crompton was persuaded not to take out a patent but to rely on the goodwill of the cotton manufacturers to repay him by subscription. Eventually they raised a paltry £60 while the mill owners got rich on his invention.

THE AUTOMATIC LOOM

The next obvious step was to mechanize weaving. The invention of the power loom came from a most unlikely source – Dr Edmund Cartwright, the rector of Goodby Marwood in Leicestershire. He invented the automatic loom for no better reason than someone had told him it was impossible, and he did so without ever having seen a handloom. He took out a patent in 1786. In the first version, the warp was held in a vertical frame and the shuttle was sent across by a powerful spring. The automatic loom was greatly improved over the years with the addition of drop boxes, each of

THE MACHINE AGE

The poet George Crabbe (1754–1852) took his wife to see one of the new textile mills. 'When she entered the building, full of engines thundering with relentless power, yet under the apparent management of children, the bare idea of the inevitable hazards attending on such stupendous undertakings quite overcame her feelings and she burst into tears.'

HOW LONG IS A PIECE OF THREAD?

'It may assist us to form a conception of the immense extent of the British cotton manufacture when it is stated that the yarn spun in this country would, in a single thread, pass round the globe's circumference 203,775 times.'

Edward Baines, *History of the Cotton Manufacture in Great Britain*, 1835

which held a shuttle with a different coloured thread. This enabled the weaver to introduce different colours into the weft by selecting the appropriate shuttle.

In the woollen industry, the fibres were often combed instead of carded. This involved pulling the wool through combs, one of which was fixed and the other held by the operator. The combs were heated by charcoal fires and, in the process, fine dust rose up from the wool. Combers rarely worked many years before lung disease brought

their careers to a tragic end. Once again Cartwright took out a patent for the first automatic machine, in 1792. By the end of the 18th century it was clear that all aspects of textile manufacture were going to be mechanized.

▲ A weaving shed photographed in 1928. The looms, each of which is powered by a belt running from overhead line shafting, would originally have been turned by a waterwheel.

◀ The arrival of complex machinery meant that large mills had to have machine shops to carry out repairs and provide replacement parts.

THE APPRENTICES

The children who worked in the new textile mills were either from local families or were sent there from the parish poor houses. Samuel Greg built Quarry Bank cotton mill at Styal, Cheshire, in 1784. He received a letter from a vicar offering to supply children, and replied that he would take young girls between nine and ten years old, but he would expect the parish to pay two guineas (£2.10) and supply them with clothes: '2 shifts, 2 frocks, 2 brats or aprons'. When they arrived they would be housed in the Apprentice House, which still stands. Today it would not be surprising to find a family home of this size: back then it held over a hundred children.

THE WORKING DAY

The mill children worked under an adult supervisor. The job was tedious and repetitive: constantly mending broken threads, taking away full bobbins and replacing them with empty ones, and cleaning away the loose cotton that continually accumulated round the machines.

The conditions in Styal were said to be particularly good, yet they seem harsh enough. One of the apprentices, 13-year-old Thomas Priestley, had a serious accident, when a finger was torn off after being caught in one of the machines. Shortly after this incident Thomas ran away, and like all runaways had to give evidence in court. Thomas reported that his working day was from six in the morning to seven in the evening. Ten minutes were allowed for breakfast that was brought to the mill, and half an hour for lunch; twice a week the lunch break was extended to an hour when the machinery was being oiled. Sometimes Thomas helped with that work and got paid a halfpenny. The apprentices had a meal in the evening, which could be no more than 'thick porridge' with water to drink, though on a Sunday they usually had boiled pork. There was no work on Sundays, but the children had to attend church in the morning and school in the afternoon. Sunday evening was the one time in the week that they could go out and play.

⋏ The apprentice house at Styal, Cheshire. In the late 18th century this was home to over a hundred girls and boys who worked in the local cotton mill.

⋏ The life of an apprentice was hard and dangerous. In this early 19th-century print a small boy can be seen in the foreground on the right, crawling among the working machinery to clean up waste.

◀ This early 19th-century cartoon, by political satirist George Cruikshank, shows overseers ill-treating apprentices in a cotton mill.

▼ Girls and boys seen here at work amongst noisy machinery in the weaving shed of a Blackburn mill, c.1900.

HARSH DISCIPLINE

Conditions were far worse in some of the other mills. The introduction of gas lighting early in the 19th century meant that mills could operate 24 hours a day. As one lot of sleepy children climbed out of bed in the morning, the night shift was ready to take their place. It was said at the time that the beds of Lancashire never got cold. The overseer who had to keep them awake sometimes could do so only by using violence. One overseer said he never wanted to hurt children – 'no man who had children of his own could bear to do it' – but admitted he sometimes felt he had no choice:

'I have kept them till ten or eleven, or sometimes twelve at night; happen once in a fortnight; beginning at six in the morning. Sometimes I might have taken the strap to them to waken them a little.'

Legislation was passed in 1819 that made it illegal to employ apprentices under the age of nine, and limited working hours to 16 per day. It had little real effect, as many mill owners were already abandoning the apprentice system. In 1822 Samuel Greg calculated that the cost of keeping apprentices had risen to five shillings (25p) a week: it was cheaper to pay a wage and let the families look after their own children.

FINED FOR HAVING FUN

Jedediah Strutt, a one-time partner of Richard Arkwright, employed apprentices at his mill in Belper, Derbyshire. Although the children were paid very little, they were still fined for any offences. The fines book reveals the children were punished for what seems harmless fun, for example: 'calling thro' the window to the Soldiers' and 'terrifying S. Pearse with her ugly face'.

A cotton mill was established on the banks of the River Clyde in 1785 and the town of New Lanark was built to house the workforce. In 1798 a 28-year-old Welshman, Robert Owen, arrived to take over the management of the mill. He had already successfully managed one in Lancashire and was full of ideas for improvements. The conditions he found were no worse than in other mills of the time, but the children were still overworked and the families, living in the tenements, demoralized. Owen began to make sweeping changes. He became a benign despot, cajoling and demanding high standards of cleanliness, honesty and sobriety. Housewives would find him appearing on their doorstep unannounced to inspect their handiwork, and he closed down the rougher pubs. But it was for his work with children that he is chiefly remembered.

AN OPPORTUNITY FOR EDUCATION

He set up a school, the New Institution, where adults and children could be taught. He recognized that young children could not be expected to learn much if they were already exhausted by working 12 or more hours a day, so he insisted that children up to the age of ten should go to school and not the mill, and the youngest infants could go to a supervised playground where, in Owen's own words, each child was to be taught 'never to injure his play-fellows but on the contrary he is to contribute all in his power to make them happy'. The children not only received the normal lessons, but were encouraged to make music and dance, and regularly gave concerts for visitors.

REVOLUTIONARY IDEAS

Owen also took the revolutionary step of reducing the working hours of all the mill hands. He reasoned that the end result of pushing workers to the point of exhaustion could only be poor workmanship and costly mistakes. He also encouraged good practices by using a system of coloured blocks at each workplace, indicating whether the individual was working

▼ The children of New Lanark putting on a dancing display for visitors at the New Institution, c. 1825.

▲ The streets of New Lanark, c.1900. The workers' tenements line the street that leads up to the count house, from which wages would have been paid out and bills settled.

FOUNDING FATHER OF SOCIALISM

Robert Owen (1771–1858) was born in Newtown, Montgomeryshire, and at the age of ten was apprenticed to a cloth merchant. The boy developed an interest in the new machinery of the cotton industry, and eventually became manager at New Lanark, where he married the owner's daughter, Caroline Dale. He became increasingly interested in socialist ideals. He dreamed of small societies, where everything would be done in a spirit of cooperation rather than competition. His attempt to found such a society in the USA at New Harmony, Indiana, ultimately failed, and the experiment cost him most of his fortune. In later life he concentrated on setting up trade unions and formed the Rational Society. He is regarded as one of the founding fathers of British socialism.

efficiently or not. His contemporaries found his ideas incomprehensible. When he was called to give evidence to the Parliamentary Committee on mill children in 1816 he explained what he had done and how productivity had increased. 'Is the committee to understand,' they asked, 'that since the first of January the machinery has been quickened? If it has not been quickened, how is it possible to state that a larger proportionable quantity has been produced?' Owen explained again, but the committee failed to understand him.

There was another innovation of Owen's that was to have widespread effects. He started a shop selling quality goods at little more than cost price, and shared out the profits with the workforce. It was to be a model for the co-operative movement. Manufacturers were slow to follow Owen's enlightened lead but the importance of what he did was recognized when New Lanark was made a World Heritage Site in 2001.

▲ A portrait of Robert Owen as a young man, by an unknown artist.

THE LUDDITES

To most people Luddites were misguided people who tried to prevent progress and preserve their traditional way of life by breaking up machinery. The real story is far more complex.

One of the first parts of the textile industry to be mechanized was the manufacture of hosiery. The Revd William Lee of Calverton, Nottinghamshire, invented his stocking frame at the end of the 16th century. According to legend he was courting a young lady who was more interested in knitting stockings than listening to his vows of undying love, so he invented a machine to take the job away from her. Soon hosiers were setting up workshops and employing workmen to use the new machines. In the 18th century the industry was governed by strict rules, which ensured that operatives went through a long apprenticeship before being allowed to work as master hosiers. But as other industries began to see apprentices merely as cheap labour, the hosiery manufacturers decided to follow suit and throw away the old rulebooks, even though they were supposed to be legally binding. In an attempt

▲ The first Luddites broke knitting frames in Nottinghamshire as a protest against their employers. This contemporary cartoon suggests a similarity to the revolutionaries of France, although this is more than a little misleading.

▼ A croppers' workshop. Croppers were among the most highly skilled and best-paid textile workers, and began machine-breaking in Yorkshire to preserve their status.

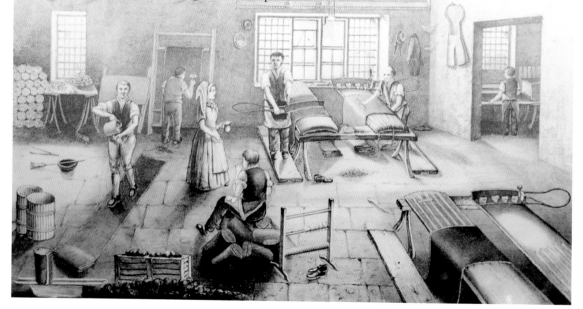

GENERAL LUDD

There was a good deal of support for the Luddites among the working population, and they were celebrated in ballads. One of these, *General Ludd's Triumph*, begins:

> *No more chant your old rhymes about bold*
>   *Robin Hood*
> *His feats I do little admire.*
> *I'll sing the achievements of General Ludd,*
> *Now the hero of Nottinghamshire.*

➤ Enoch's hammer:
this was the hammer used
to break cropping frames made by
Enoch Taylor. It is now preserved in
the Tolson Museum, Huddersfield.

the cry 'Enoch has made 'em and Enoch'll break 'em'. Events became ever more violent. A number of croppers died when attacking the mills and a crisis-point was reached on 28 April when the most prominent of the manufacturers who used shearing frames, William Horsfall, was shot and killed. Three men – George Mellor, William Thorpe and Thomas Smith – were brought to court as ringleaders and found guilty of the murder. All three were hanged and the judge imposed the extra ruling that their bodies should be sent for dissection. The Luddite rebellion was over.

to force their masters to obey the laws, the knitters applied to the courts and petitioned Parliament – but without success. In desperation they decided that the only way to make the employers take notice was to smash their frames and destroy their profits. The machine-breaking began in 1811, and to preserve the anonymity and avoid prosecution, they invented a fictitious leader known either as General Ludd or Ned Ludd. Ultimately they failed and the regulations that had protected employees were scrapped.

THE CROPPERS' REVOLT

The Nottingham Luddites were not objecting to the use of machinery – the stocking frame had already been in use for well over a century when the machine-breaking began. The story of what happened in Yorkshire the following year is very different. The croppers here were the elite of the cloth trade. Their job of finishing the cloth by trimming the nap with heavy shears was not only physically demanding but required great precision if the material was not to be ruined. It was inevitable that the process would eventually be mechanized, but the shearing frames were introduced at a time of high unemployment. The croppers began machine-breaking in 1812. Many of the cropping frames were made by Enoch Taylor of Marsden in West Yorkshire, and the Luddites broke them with 'Enoch's hammer', with

REWARDS.

WHEREAS, two Villains did, on the Night of Wednesday the 22nd. Day of July Instant, feloniously SHOOT at and WOUND *John Hinchliffe*, of *Upper Thong*, in the West Riding of the County of York, Clothier, with intent to MURDER him, of which Wound he lies in a dangerous state.

A Reward of 200 Guineas

will be given to any Person who will give such Information, as may lead to the Apprehenfion and Conviction of either of the said Villains.

AND WHEREAS, John Scholefield Junior, of Nether-Thong, in the said Riding, is strongly suspected of being concerned in the said Murderous attempt, AND HAS ABSCONDED.

A Reward of Twenty Guineas

IS HEREBY OFFERED TO ANY Person, who will apprehend the said John Scholefield, and lodge him in any of his Majesty's Prisons, and give Information thereof, or give such Private Information as may lead to his apprehenfion; *and Invictable Secrecy will be Observed.*

The said John Scholefield is by Trade a Cloth-Dresser, about 21 Years of Age, 5 Feet 10 Inches High, Brown Hair, Dark Complexion, rather stout made: commonly wears a Dark coloured Coat, made rather short, and Lead coloured Jean Pantaloons.

The above Rewards will be paid upon fuch Information, Apprehenfion, and Conviction as above mentioned by

Mr. John Peace, of Huddersfield,

in the said County of York, Treasurer to the Huddersfield Association.

▲ A reward poster of 1812, featuring one of the many attacks on clothiers by Luddites.

POWER FOR THE MILLS

The first generation of textile mills relied on the waterwheel for power. There was an inescapable problem with the system: in times of drought the wheel might be stopped. The first steam engines were introduced early in the 18th century for pumping water from mines, and they found a limited use with watermills as well. They could pump water from the tail-race, when it had passed the wheel, and return it back to the millpond or leat above the wheel to be used again.

THE INTRODUCTION OF STEAM

The early steam engines were more properly called atmospheric engines. They had open-topped cylinders and the steam was passed into the cylinder then condensed by spraying with cold water, creating a vacuum. Air pressure then acted on the piston to force it down the cylinder. It was James Watt (1736–1819) who turned the atmospheric engine into a true steam engine, by using the expansion of steam in a closed cylinder to act on the piston. This meant that the piston could now be pushed up as well as being forced down,

▲ The earliest steam engines used in mills were beam engines. This example, which was built around 1840, is now part of the Northern Mill Engine Society's magnificent collection.

▼ The beam engine gave way to ever more powerful horizontal engines, such as this immense compound engine that was installed at Dee Mill at Shaw, Lancashire, in 1907.

∧ The arrival of steam power released mill owners from the constraints of building by running water. In this photograph, mills line the canal in Skipton, Yorkshire, and the terraced houses for mill workers climb the hillside behind them.

and it was a comparatively simple matter to turn this up and down motion into rotary motion: the engine could turn the wheels of a mill.

The first rotative steam engine was installed at Robinson's textile mill at Papplewick, Nottinghamshire, in 1788. The use of steam power spread rapidly, especially in the north of England. Over the years the engines were greatly improved and became ever more powerful. Single cylinder engines gave way to compound engines, in which the steam passed from one cylinder to another; these giants could power every machine in even the biggest mill. The huge engine at Trencherfield Mill, Wigan, for example, has a rating of 2,500 horsepower. It was James Watt himself who first introduced the term 'horsepower', which literally referred to the work that could be done by one horse. The men who looked after these great machines were always immensely proud of

their charges. All the brass work was kept shining brightly, paintwork gleamed and the engine man was master of his domain. No one dreamed of entering without permission, no matter what their status in the company.

The arrival of the steam engine did more than increase efficiency: it brought about a fundamental change in the way in which the industry was organized. As long as manufacturers had to rely on the waterwheel they were limited to where they could site their factories. With that restriction gone, mills could be sited alongside the transport routes that would bring in the raw materials and the coal to fire the boilers for the new engines. At first this meant that canalside sites were very much in favour, and along the Leeds & Liverpool Canal, for example, are areas where the mills crowd together along the banks. With no restrictions, mills could be set close together and what had once been mill villages became mill towns. New machines and steam power brought huge increases in production. In 1791, when steam was a novelty, Britain imported two million pounds (900 tonnes) in weight of raw cotton: by the 1830s this had risen to an amazing 400 million pounds (180,000 tonnes) a year.

SPINNERS

A spinner repairing a broken thread on a spinning mule.

mill construction, in spite of the expense. In 1818 Samuel Greg built an extension to the existing mill at Styal, installing more waterframes with a total of 3,000 new spindles at a cost of £11,764. But they were doing the work of 3,000 traditional spinners: it could pay for itself in a year.

The introduction of spinning machines did not necessarily mean that life was easier for the operatives, as the children working in Arkwright's mill discovered. In 1835, Andrew Ure wrote *The Philosophy of Manufacture* in praise of the factory system; he declared that all the changes were 'philanthropic' and that 'at every step of each manufacturing process described in this volume, the humanity of science will be manifest.' But even

▼ A doffer at work, removing the full bobbins from a mule.

As late as the end of the 18th century, most of the carding and spinning in the woollen industry was still carried out by women working at home. Thomas Crossley of Bradford had a network of spinners working for him on a regular basis: 'We had spinning done in Lancashire, as far as Ormskirk; in Craven, and at Kirby Lonsdale; in Wensleydale, Swaledale and other parts of North Yorkshire.' He estimated that a good spinner could earn two shillings and sixpence (12.5p) a week – but there was a problem. Although the wool that was distributed around the areas all came from the same batch, the yarn produced by one spinner could be a very different thickness from that produced by another. Machine spinning, when it was introduced, removed that difficulty as well as being more efficient. It was just one more reason to make the investment in

▲ Spinning mules in a Gloucestershire woollen mill.

he had to admit that not everything was perfect: 'Arkwright's waterframes were built very low in the spindle box to accommodate children, and consequently sometimes caused deformity.'

The waterframe was not suitable for the woollen industry, but the introduction of the spinning mule brought mechanization to all parts of the textile world. The mule was greatly improved by Manchester loom manufacturer Richard Roberts in 1825, and the machines got far bigger than Crompton's original, with later examples having as many as 1,200 spindles.

DANGEROUS WORK

In the 19th century, a minder would have charge of a pair of mules and two children would be employed as 'piecers'. Their job was to mend broken threads. It was usual for three or four threads to break every minute, and the piecers had to tie them together. It was a tricky job, because they were dealing with a machine with moving parts. There were only a few seconds pause each time the carriage moved backwards and forwards.

It was tiring work, spending all day walking to and fro with the carriage. Cleaning was an even more dangerous business. A large amount of fluff was created that had to be cleared from the mechanism at regular intervals. The mules were briefly stopped, and a child would rush down the length of the mule under the threads. Sometimes the overseer would restart a mule while the child was still there, and he or she would be crushed.

Once all the spindles were full, the machine had to be stopped. The full bobbins were removed and empty ones inserted by the doffers. Speed was essential: while the mule was stationary it was not earning money. As one operative said, you never had to worry about exercise and slimming if you were a mule spinner.

In spite of the development of power looms at the end of the 18th century, handlooms were still in use well into the next century, but times were increasingly hard for the weavers. William Varley, a Lancashire weaver, kept diaries for a number of years. On 8 January 1820 he wrote: 'A great talk of an advance of wages which was to take place this day, but all is a mistake. Alas, poor weaver, thy fond hopes of better days always prove abortive; distress and scorn is thy true companions; thy haggard and meagre looks plainly indicate thy hard usage and slavery, which knows no bounds.'

Over the next few years conditions got steadily worse and by 1827 Varley was reporting that 'the pox and measles takes off the children by two or three a house; and well may they die, for there is no aid, no succour to be had for them'. His problem was that when power looms came in, his skills were no longer needed as increasingly the work went to women and girls. Edward Baines, who wrote a history of the cotton industry in 1835, explained just what was happening. He estimated

▲ Preparing the warp threads, which are being arranged in the correct order on a warping frame.

that an experienced adult handloom weaver could produce two lengths of shirting a week, but by 1823 a 15-year-old steam-loom weaver could look after two looms and produce seven pieces. Ten years later that same weaver, with the assistance of a 12-year-old girl, could produce 20 pieces on four looms. The demise of handloom weaving was inevitable, but was not accepted quietly.

RIOTS

During the late 1820s and into the 1830s there were outbreaks of rioting, in which power looms were smashed throughout the textile districts. In Glasgow in 1831 it was the women who led

▲ A typical weaving shed at the beginning of the 20th century: the north-facing rooflights provided a good, even illumination.

A HAND LOOM WEAVER'S LAMENT

Come all you cotton-weavers, your looms you must pull down:
You must be employ'd in factories, in country or in town,
For our cotton-masters have found out a wonderful new scheme,
These calico goods now wove by hand they're going to weave by steam.

A verse from a 19th-century broadsheet ballad

▲ A weaver repairing a broken warp thread.

the way. The local paper reported how 'several hundreds of honest wives and bonny lasses' gathered at McArthur's factory to inform him that they would not injure him, provided he allowed them to smash the machines. He gave in, or as the paper put it, 'was not so ungallant and uncivil as to refuse compliance with the pressing requests or peremptory demands of the fair sex as had honoured him with a visit'. But machine-breaking could never halt the march of mechanization.

HIGH-SPEED SHUTTLES

Although the looms may have been mechanized, the job of warping – arranging the warp threads onto a beam that was set in place on the loom – had

▲ Some mills specialized in particular cloths. This weaver at Cam Mill, Gloucestershire, in the 1940s is working at a broad loom, producing cloth for billiard tables.

scarcely changed. Life in the weaving shed, however, was very different from the old days. The first thing that struck any visitor was the almost unbearable racket of hundreds of shuttles being banged backwards and forwards at high speed. The weavers' main tasks were watching for broken threads and regularly replacing the weft in the shuttles. One weaver described it as a dangerous affair, because even in the early 20th century there were seldom any guards in place and it was easy for a shuttle to fly out: 'I'd often be walking down the middle of the loom shop when a shuttle'd come whizzing past my head.' At least the arrival of the new shuttleless looms in modern times removed that danger.

FINISHING THE CLOTH

For centuries woollen cloth had been fulled at special fulling mills, but these were gradually replaced by milling machines, in which the wet cloth was squeezed between rollers. A length of cloth had to have the ends sewn together to make a loop, so that it could be kept going round and round through the rollers for many hours. Large industrial sewing machines and heavy thread were used, and one unfortunate worker at a Gloucestershire mill, who was tending two sewing machines at the same time, put a needle right through his finger. Someone had to fetch a spanner to release the needle while another colleague went to get him a cup of tea. The man who brought the spanner fainted at the sight so he was given the tea instead of the victim. When the injured worker was released he went to the local hospital to have the needle removed, but insisted on having it back because it was 'company property'. No one could ever be quite certain where hazards might appear next in a textile mill.

DYEING

If the wool had not been dyed before spinning, it would often be dyed 'in the piece', either in the mill or in a separate dye works. One mill manager described the local dye works as being like a scene from Dante's 'Inferno': 'Men stripped to the waist, wearing loin cloths and with long beards, poling

▲ After weaving, woollen cloth was cleaned and shrunk in milling machines such as these, that replaced old fulling stocks.

▼ To raise the nap the cloth runs over the teasels in a continuous loop, as seen here in this gig mill.

▲ The teasel heads are put in place in batons which are then set on the rotating drum of a teasel gig mill.

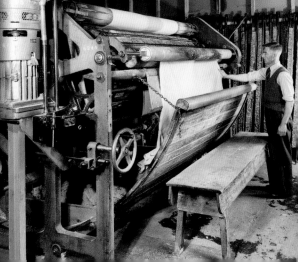

▲ Before being despatched, cloth was inspected in rooms with good, natural light.

➤ After inspection, any faults had to be repaired by a delicate hand.

vats of indigo heated on open fires.' Some areas specialized in dyeing. Stroud in Gloucestershire was famous for its scarlet cloth that was made for uniforms for the British Army.

COMPLETING THE NAP

Among the final processes involved in finishing woollen cloth were the raising and trimming of the nap. The teasel raising gig mill used a circular drum, with batons of teasel heads on the outside. As the cloth ran over the rotating drum, the barbs on the teasels pulled up the fibres. The nap could then be cut, in later years using rotating blades – a device that inspired Edwin Budding of Stroud to invent the lawnmower in 1830.

INSPECTION

When all the various processes that started with a bale of cotton or wool and ended with a length of cloth were complete, there was still one vital stage to go through: the cloth had to be inspected and any faults repaired. The atmosphere in the inspection area was very different from that of the rest of a mill. The rooms needed to be well lit and the absence of noisy machinery ensured a more peaceful scene. The cloth could either be inspected by being hung vertically over rollers in a good light or placed on a flat table, where a sense of touch was as important as good eyesight in detecting flaws. A delicate touch was also needed in making repairs so that the finished cloth appeared absolutely perfect.

PRINTING ON COTTON

Cotton cloth was often printed with patterns that could be quite complex. Originally, this was done using wooden blocks onto which the pattern was carved by hand, a job that required considerable skill. The block would be covered with a mordant that fixed the dye and pressed against the cloth, which was then immersed in the dye vat. Only the areas that had been treated with the mordant retained the colour. Later the process was mechanized using engraved copper rollers in place of the old wooden blocks.

SILK MILLS

◄ Women control silk threads being wound onto reels, turned by the system of pulleys running from the shaft rotated by the man on the left.

Silk weaving was first introduced into Britain by Huguenot refugees, who fled France when the Edict of Nantes was revoked in 1685 and Protestantism was made illegal. The weavers mostly settled in the Spitalfields district of London, where they worked in garrets. Their houses are still easily recognized by the large windows of the workrooms at the top of the buildings.

THE LOMBE BROTHERS

Silk thread was mainly imported from Italy, where they had developed a machine for 'throwing' silk – twisting the delicate threads together to make a yarn. A London merchant, Thomas Lombe, was determined to discover the secret of how it was done and sent his brother, John, to Piedmont, now part of Italy, disguised as an itinerant workman. John saw the machines, made secret drawings and smuggled them back to England in 1717. The Lombe brothers built a mill in Derby and installed the machinery. The story, however, takes a sinister turn: John Lombe died in 1722 in mysterious circumstances, and it was said that he had been poisoned by the Piedmontese as revenge for stealing their secrets. Nevertheless, silk mills soon proliferated and Macclesfield, Cheshire, became a major centre for the industry.

THE DRAW BOY'S TASK

Silk was a luxury and the highest prices were paid for cloth woven with intricate patterns. Producing these patterns was a highly complex affair, involving raising and lowering the different warp threads in the right order, a job that fell to the draw boy. Originally he stood at the side of the loom, but as patterns became ever more complex he had to take a precarious perch on top of the machine. The warp threads passed through wire loops, known as healds. To take a simple example, supposing the warp threads are all red and the weft all blue: if the boy lifted a heald, the blue thread would pass under it and the red thread would appear on top and show in the finished fabric; conversely, if it remained down the blue would show.

A VERY SPECIAL MATERIAL

Silk is produced as part of the life cycle of the silk moth. The pupa is wrapped in filaments to form a cocoon: seen under a microscope, these filaments have a triangular cross-section, so that each thread acts as a long prism, scattering the light, and it is this that gives silk its special lustre.

▲ Weaving silk on a Jacquard loom in Essex: the punched cards control the movement of the warp threads; the shuttle is being passed by hand.

Geoff Hide, whose family owned Whitchurch Silk Mill in Hampshire from 1886 to 1955, recounts this story: 'Rita Bingham was born in Whitchurch. Her father died in 1927 when she was 14 and she went to the silk mill for a job but the owner, my great uncle James Hide, did not have any work for her until the following year. She trained as a winder and after 12 months was allowed to warp. She earned 10 shillings (50p) a week, though unknown to the other girls James gave her an extra half a crown (12.5p) as she was supporting her widowed mother. Rita started weaving when she was 17, working from 8a.m. to 7p.m. and initially earning 4d (2p) per yard – a job she continued to do until she retired in the mid 1980s.'

THE JACQUARD LOOM

Joseph Marie Jacquard of Lyon in France had experienced the misery of toiling for up to ten hours a day in the cramped position of the draw boy, and he was determined that others should be spared the pain. In 1801 he invented a system using punched cards, whereby the order in which healds were raised depended on whether or not they could pass through one of the holes in the card, or were stopped by hitting a blank section. The card was automatically moved into place for each throw of the shuttle.

▲ Rita Bingham (second right), aged 15, stands alongside James Hide, who owned Whitchurch Silk Mill until his death in his 90th year.

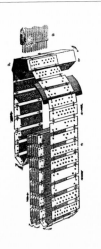

◄ Cards for a Jacquard loom: the arrangement of the holes determines the pattern to be woven.

The Jacquard loom was, in effect, the first computerized machine, with the cards having a simple digital code – lift or no lift. Thanks to these inventions, textile manufacturing completed the move from the home to the factory.

25

MILL TOWNS

When the arrival of steam power liberated manufacturers from the need to site their mills beside running water, many of the old country mills were abandoned and new mills were built close together to take advantage of the best transport routes. As workers wanted to be as near to the mills as possible, speculative builders were soon putting up rows of cheap housing. Many of the houses were built in long terraces as back-to-backs, which were just what the name suggests. Because of the way they were built there could be no rear gardens or yards, and most houses fronted directly onto the streets. Many of these homes were often built under the tall shadow of the multi-storey mill.

Change was slow to come to some of the older textile areas, such as Gloucestershire, but in Lancashire and Yorkshire towns grew at a remarkable rate. Some towns, such as Manchester, could not keep up with the swelling population, and as a result people crowded into whatever accommodation they could find, no matter how

THE CAMPAIGNING DOCTOR

Scotsman John Ferriar (1761–1815), a physician at Manchester Infirmary at the end of the 18th century, recognized that atrocious living conditions bred disease, especially in cheap lodging houses: 'The horror of these houses cannot easily be described; a lodger fresh from the country often lies down in a bed, filled with infection from the last tenant, or from which the corpse of a victim to fever has only been removed a few hours before.' His research led to the introduction of many sanitary reforms, and he was instrumental in setting up the Board of Health.

squalid. The 24-year-old son of a German cotton manufacturer was sent to Manchester by his father to study English technology and he was appalled by the conditions he found. His name was Frederick Engels and he wrote about what he saw in *The Condition of the English Working Class* (1845). He described the labyrinth of courtyards close to the River Irk, itself 'a narrow coal-black, foul-smelling stream, full of debris and refuse'. Here were houses without either stone or wood floors, with broken

▼ At the beginning of the 20th century, conditions in the slums of Manchester, like these at Newgates, Corporation Street, were as bad as they had ever been.

▲ Sir Titus Salt built a mill and a whole new town of decent houses that he named Saltaire.

➤ The houses in Newgates in Manchester had few facilities and new arrivals had to crowd together in common lodging houses.

windows and doors. 'Everywhere heaps of debris, refuse, and offal, standing pools and gutters, and a stench which alone would make it impossible for a human being in any degree civilized to live there.' But people did live there, in their thousands.

SALT'S MODEL TOWN

Bradford in Yorkshire was little better than Manchester, and one local manufacturer decided to provide something better for himself and his workforce. Sir Titus Salt had purchased 500 bales of alpaca wool, imported to Liverpool from South America, in 1836, which no one else seemed to want. According to Charles Dickens, writing in *Household Words*, it consisted of 'a huge pile of dirty looking sacks with some fibrous material which had a strong resemblance to superannuated horsehair or frowsy, elongated wool'. The fibres, however, were lustrous, and when Salt had worked out how to spin it economically he decided to build a new factory. He chose a site beside the River Aire, well away from the smoke and grime of Bradford, and there he built his mill and a new town: Saltaire. The houses were of a high quality and over the years he provided many facilities – schools, a church, a hospital and almshouses. One thing the town did not have was a pub. Salt did not want anyone to have a place to meet to discuss matters such as wages and plan strikes. He even went so far as to enforce rules that included: 'Gathering of eight or more people in streets is strictly forbidden.' He was undoubtedly philanthropic, but also strict and dictatorial.

In the 18th century the concept of leisure time for mill workers scarcely existed. It was considered quite normal for people to work 12 hours a day for six days of the week, though not everyone agreed with this concept. John Fielden had a cotton mill in Todmorden, Lancashire, but had a passionate interest in politics and in 1832 was elected as MP for Oldham with a fellow radical, William Cobbett. Together they campaigned for a Ten Hour Bill to limit working hours, but not even other radically inclined politicians, such as Joseph Hume, supported them. Hume's view was typical of opinion at the time: 'All legislative interference must be pernicious. Men must be left to themselves to make their own contracts.' Fielden never gave up and the Ten Hour Act was finally passed in 1847. It was the start of a process that was eventually to lead to the acknowledgement that factory workers should be legally entitled to a holiday.

SPORTING FACILITIES

By the latter part of the 19th century, as more leisure time became available, industrialists were beginning to recognize that supporting activities for their workforce was a good thing, not just for raising morale but also for improving health. Sir Titus Salt, for example, provided a park where sports could be played. One sport that gained great popularity in Lancashire and Yorkshire was cricket. The Lancashire League was founded in the 1880s and began the move towards professionalism, by allowing two members of the team to be paid. As a result, local clubs would eventually field sides with famous international players, such as the West Indian Learie Constantine, who joined the Nelson club in the 1920s.

BRASS BANDS

Another great tradition that developed in the northern towns was that of the brass band. One of the most famous of them all was formed mainly from workers at Black Dyke Mills in Queensbury, Yorkshire, in 1855. They were a great

⌃ Music-making was popular among mill workers. The kazoo band from William Playne's mill in Gloucestershire displays proudly the trophy they won in 1936.

➤ Even comparatively small mills organized works outings: this Gloucestershire group posing in front of their coach have dressed in their best clothes for the occasion.

WAKES WEEK IN BLACKPOOL

'Every train brings huge crowds of them, with carpet bags, boxes, and bundle handkerchiefs, which they carry to their lodgings. These people mean business, and intend to play at least a week.'

Pall Mall Magazine, 1884

advertisement for the company, wearing smart uniforms made from cloth woven at the mill. Not everyone could afford expensive instruments, so in the early 20th century there was a vogue for kazoo marching bands.

▲ Blackpool was a favourite resort for Lancashire Wakes Week. Here the excited crowds arrive at the railway station.

WAKES WEEK

A much-treasured institution was the Wakes holiday, based on an old religious celebration dating back many centuries. In the 19th century it developed into Wakes Week, when throughout the textile districts of the north, mills would close down. It was usual for each town to choose a different week and then for every mill in that town to close. For the workers it was an unpaid holiday; for the mill owners an opportunity to catch up on maintenance and repairs. The spread of the rail system made it possible for families to travel and seaside resorts prospered – none more so than Blackpool, where the first station opened in 1846.

That same year the town also got its first pier and over time more amenities were added. The opening of the famous Tower in 1894 helped to consolidate the town's position as the favourite resort for Lancashire mill workers.

➤ In this photograph, taken from the top of Blackpool Tower in 1938, the beach is almost invisible under the mass of bodies.

MILL BUILDINGS

The earliest mill buildings were massive for their time, rising five or six storeys high, and dominating the surrounding houses. Their owners tried to make them seem not too daunting by decking them out with architectural details, such as prominent pediments, in an attempt to make them look like rather plain country mansions. There was one feature that almost invariably had a prominent position: the bell tower. In an age when the poor could seldom afford a clock, it was the bell that summoned them to work and told them when they could leave. Anyone who arrived after the bell had finished tolling would either find the doors shut in their face, or they would be allowed in but forfeit as much as half a day's pay for being a couple of minutes late.

The aristocracy tended to regard the arrival of these new buildings with contempt. John Byng, Viscount Torrington, visited Cromford, and in his diary of 1792 noted: 'Every rural sound is sunk in the clamour of cotton works; and the simple peasant changed into the impudent artisan.' But even he was impressed with the mills when gas lighting was introduced, comparing them to a man-of-war, 'and, when they are lighted up on a dark night, look most luminously beautiful'.

NO HEALTH AND SAFETY

Inside the mills, the drive had to be taken from the waterwheel or steam engine through a system known as line shafting. The shafts ran right through the mill, connected to each other through gears. Pulleys on the shafts were attached to the machines down below by leather belts. There were no guardrails, so these represented a real hazard for the workers: anyone caught up by a belt would risk being carried along by it and crushed.

There was another, far greater hazard connected with the old mills: fire. The combination of inflammable material – such as cotton waste, hot oil and grease – and the friction from moving machinery was a potentially disastrous mixture. In 1803, North Mill at Belper, Derbyshire, went up in flames, destroying a lot of valuable machinery, none of which was insured. When the mill was rebuilt it was very different from its predecessor. At its heart was a rigid iron frame of pillars and beams, with the beams joined together by low-rise brick arches. Iron ties held the pillars together to resist the thrust of the arches.

▲ North Mill in Belper, Derbyshire, built in 1804 to house the cotton spinning machinery invented by Sir Richard Arkwright, is an early example of a fireproof building. This cutaway diagram shows the waterwheel and the method of transmitting the power to the different parts of the mill.

▲ Like many early textile mills, Hampshire's Whitchurch Silk Mill, built in 1815, has the restrained elegance of Georgian architecture.

➤ At work in the manager's imposing office at Ham Mill, Gloucestershire, c.1950.

The floors were then laid over these arches. That was not the only innovation: down in the basement was a stove, from which the hot air rose through flues to all the upper floors. North Mill was centrally heated.

TIMES OF CHANGE

The arrival of steam engines and power looms brought the final changes to the mills. The tall chimneys appeared that were to be the most significant feature of many mill towns. Weaving sheds were added as single-storey buildings, lit by distinctive windows set into the north-facing sides of multi-pitched roofs. Over the years, mills simply got bigger and bigger: John Crossley's Dean Clough Mill in Halifax, Yorkshire, for example, was employing 5,000 people by the end of the 19th century. The buildings are still there but, like so many former textile mills, their old working life is over and they have a new role as an arts and conference centre and offices, while other mills have become museums or been turned into luxury apartments. Some mills have survived by finding niche markets. In Gloucestershire, for example, mills in Stroud and Cam are the world's leading manufacturers of billiard-table cloth, while Whitchurch Silk Mill in Hampshire has often been called upon to provide authentic materials for costume dramas, including television progammes such as *Pride and Prejudice* and *Cranford*. There may be far fewer mills than there were in the past, but their work goes on and remains an important, living part of Britain's heritage.

PLACES TO VISIT

Britain has many mills that are open to visitors and provide fascinating insights into their history. The mills, museums and visitor centres listed below are just some of those that are well worth a visit. Contact the sites or visit their websites for further information, including details of opening dates and times.

Armley Mills: Leeds Industrial Museum, Canal Road, Armley, Leeds LS2 2QF

Bancroft Mill Engine Trust, Gillians Lane, Barnoldswick, Lancashire BB18 5QR

Blackburn Museum, Museum Street, Blackburn, Lancashire BB1 7AJ

Bolton Steam Museum, Atlas Mills, Chorley Old Road, Bolton, Lancashire BL1 4EU

Bradford Industrial Museum, Moorside Mills, Moorside Road, Eccleshill, Bradford, West Yorkshire BD2 3HP

Coldharbour Mill, Uffculme, Cullompton, Devon EX15 3EE

Colne Valley Museum, Cliffe Ash, Golcar, Huddersfield, West Yorkshire HD7 4PY

Cotswold Woollen Weavers, Filkins, near Lechlade, Gloucestershire GL7 3JJ

Cromford Mill, Mill Lane, Cromford, Matlock, Derbyshire DE4 3RQ

Derby Silk Mill, Silk Mill Lane, Derby, Derbyshire DE1 3AF

Dunkirk Mill Centre, Nailsworth, Gloucestershire GL5 5HH

Ellenroad Engine House, Elizabeth Way, Newhey, Rochdale, Lancashire OL16 4LE

Hall i'th' Wood Museum, Green Way, off Crompton Way, Bolton, Greater Manchester BL1 8UA

Helmshore Mills Textile Museum, Holcombe Road, Helmshore, Rossendale, Lancashire BB4 4NP

Islay Woollen Mill, Bridgend, Isle of Islay, Inner Hebrides, Scotland PA44 7PG

Macclesfield Silk Museums, The Heritage Centre, Roe Street, Macclesfield, Cheshire SK11 6UT

Masson Mills, Derby Road, Matlock Bath, Derbyshire DE4 3PY

Museum in the Park, Stratford Park, Stroud, Gloucestershire GL5 4AF

National Wool Museum, Dre-Fach Felindre, Llandysul, Carmarthenshire, Wales SA44 5UP

New Lanark World Heritage Site and Visitor Centre, New Lanark, South Lanarkshire, Scotland ML11 9DB

Newtown Textile Museum, 5–7 Commercial Street, Newtown, Powys, Wales SY16 2BL

North Mill, Bridgefoot, Belper, Derbyshire DE56 1YD

Nottingham Industrial Museum, Wollaton Hall, Wollaton, Nottingham, Nottinghamshire NG8 2AE

Paisley Thread Mill Museum, Mile End Mill, Seedhill Road, Paisley, Renfrewshire, Scotland PA1 1JS

Quarry Bank Mill and Styal Estate, Styal, Wilmslow, Cheshire SK9 4LA

Queen Street Mill Textile Museum, Harle Syke, Burnley, Lancashire BB10 2HX

Robert Owen Museum, The Cross, Broad Street, Newtown, Powys, Wales SY16 2BB

Rock Mill, Capel Dewi, Llandysul, Ceredigion, Carmarthenshire, Wales SA44 4PH

Ruddington Framework Knitters' Museum, Chapel Street, Ruddington, Nottingham, Nottinghamshire NG11 6HE

Salts Mill, Shipley, Saltaire, West Yorkshire BD18 3LA

Scotland's Jute Museum @ Verdant Works, West Henderson's Wynd, Dundee, Scotland DD1 5BT

Shetland Textile Working Museum, Böd of Gremista, Gremista, Lerwick, Shetland, Scotland ZE1 0PX

Silk Industry Museum, Park Lane, Macclesfield, Cheshire SK11 6TJ

Tolson Museum, Ravensknowle Park, Wakefield Road, Huddersfield, West Yorkshire HD5 8DJ

Trefriw Woollen Mills, Main Road, Trefriw, Conwy Valley, North Wales LL27 0NQ

Weaver's Cottage, The Cross, Shuttle Street, Kilbarchan, Renfewshire, Scotland PA10 2JG

Whitchurch Silk Mill, Winchester Street, Whitchurch, Hampshire RG28 7AL

Information correct at time of going to press.

▲ Masson Mills in Derbyshire. This is a fine example of an Arkwright cotton mill, part of which is now a working textile museum.